CHRIST OUR LIGHT

CHRIST OUR LIGHT

PRAYING WITH REMBRANDT'S ETCHINGS OF THE LIFE OF CHRIST

From the Collection in the National Gallery of Victoria
Selected with a Commentary by ANNE MARGOT BOYD

CANTERBURY
PRESS
Norwich

First published in 2005 by the Canterbury Press Norwich
(a publishing imprint of Hymns Ancient & Modern Limited,
a registered charity)
9-17 St Albans Place, London N1 0NX

www.scm-canterburypress.co.uk

British Library Cataloguing in Publication data

A catalogue record for this book is available
from the British Library

ISBN 1-85311-649-1

Design by Lynne Muir
Typeset by JamesGrechDesign
Printed and bound by Tien Wah, Singapore

Contents

Foreword

With *Christ Our Light* Anne Boyd takes us on a spiritual journey. Accompanied by Rembrandt's etchings we become like the by-standers and followers of Christ shown in those images. We too are invited – through Anne's insightful engagement with the prints – to encounter the Gospel narrative with freshness and immediacy. This book shows us both the genius of Rembrandt's artistry and the wisdom of his religious insight.

If one surveys the bibliography that Rembrandt has inspired, one sees that the Dutch artist has stimulated art historians and theologians alike. Every generation of religious seekers, it seems, has turned to Rembrandt's work (especially the etchings), sensing that these small objects grew out of profound spiritual questioning. They make the Gospels resound to our own searching.

In the past scholars have puzzled over the question of Rembrandt's own religious and spiritual commitment. Unfortunately, written sources provide us with very little direct evidence of Rembrandt's religious sensibility. As a result, many scholars have abstained from speculating about this aspect of the artist's life. But Anne Boyd shows us a different way to approach Rembrandt's inner life through the parallels that she draws between the Gospel narratives and Rembrandt's known experiences. We have only to gaze at an etching such as *The Return of the Prodigal Son* to realise how deeply and compulsively this man searched for meaning in favourite incidents from the Gospels.

'Deeply' and 'compulsively': these terms apply equally well to the intensity with which Rembrandt performed the physical process of print-making. During Rembrandt's lifetime it was unusual for an artist of his calibre to prepare the copper plate himself. Most of his contemporaries would have provided a drawing, whose transfer to a plate they might or might not have supervised. Rembrandt by way of contrast worked and reworked his own plates. As a result of his unflagging attentiveness, he made the pictorial demands of each narrative quite literally stand out on the paper. Not only do fine networks of lines (known as 'hatching'), as well as deliberate contrasts of areas of light and shade (known as 'chiaroscuro') provide the visual means by which dramatic narratives are communicated, but the lines themselves are dug into the plate with varying degrees of force so as to express emotional nuances in Rembrandt's interpretation of individual scenes. The physicality of gouging copper – whether by metal burin as in engraving or by drawing with a needle in a wax coating as in etching – leaves its mark on the page. Anne Boyd guides us into a world of Christian vision evoked by patterns of black lines on white paper resulting from labouring over a copper plate.

Occasionally someone looking at these etchings may voice disquiet that the figures or the setting may not show fidelity to the historicity of a Biblical scene. How can we know that the artist has imagined scenes as they might actually have looked? The answer is that we can't. Instead Anne Boyd helps us to grasp that rather than weakening the power of an event as in say *Christ Presented to the People*, Rembrandt's ability to insert a Biblical narrative into a recognisable seventeenth-century setting serves to insert us into the narrative as well. Rembrandt puts us in the picture of how Christ preached and prayed, and Anne Boyd invites us to enter with her into that miracle.

CLAIRE RENKIN
Yarra Theological Union

Introduction

Rembrandt's etchings first came to my attention in 1969 when the British Museum mounted an exhibition of the famous Dutch artist's etchings of the life of Christ. The exhibition brought together, in one long gallery, prints, plates and tools to show not only the whole process of etching but also Rembrandt's various etchings of the same subject. He often worked over a particular etching, making changes that become apparent as successive prints are displayed side by side. The exhibition catalogue pointed out that never since Rembrandt made the prints would so many have appeared in one place. They were unlikely to do so again.

At the time I had been working as a letterpress printer and was also familiar with the practice of meditation, the purpose for which many of the etchings were made. It is not surprising that the day spent in that London gallery has stayed in my memory. Another exhibition, this time in the National Gallery of Victoria in Melbourne in 1998, reminded me again of Rembrandt's etchings. The exhibition, *Beyond Belief: Modern Art and the Religious Imagination*, concentrated on modern religious works but, almost as an introduction, displayed a few of the gallery's permanent collection of Rembrandt's etchings of the life of Christ.

I had to wait until 2003, when the gallery reopened after renovations, to see more of their etchings and make the selection for this book. Now I offer it, simply to share the beauty, the spiritual heights and depths, of these masterpieces of religious art.

Experiencing God in the Story of Jesus

Rembrandt was working in a long tradition of Eastern and Western Christian artists who made images of Jesus that reveal him as Emmanuel, as 'God with us'. The Divine Being, God as Word and Life and Light, is revealed in the person of Jesus Christ and in the stories he told and embodied. The words and the stories were recorded in the Gospels. Visual images have survived: in scenes painted on the walls of burial places, carved on tombs and wrought in mosaic on the walls of churches. They also appeared in books.

From the sixth century we have fragments of illustrated Books of the Gospels, showing scenes such as the Raising of Lazarus and the Healing of the Blind Man. The aim was to invite the reader to engage more deeply in the meaning of the Jesus story. Although from time to time the use of images was prohibited (lest they be worshipped instead of God), this rich tradition has continued into the present, with artists using their skills and vision to enable us to 'see Jesus'. They are not trying to depict God - an impossibility - or simply to show the 'human side' of Jesus. They show us a human life radiating the light and force, the energy of God.

Using visual images in prayer

When an artist approaches the making of an image of Christ in a spirit of prayer and reverence, as do the makers of icons in the Eastern tradition and, I believe, as Rembrandt must have done, the result is an image that invites us to open ourselves to God's action. Such an invitation – to let God transform us through our contemplation of a prayerful image – is similar to opening ourselves to the word of God in meditative reading of the Bible. This is especially true in the practice known as *lectio divina* or 'holy reading'. *Lectio divina* is a slow, meditative, daily reading of the Bible, usually in short passages, where the reader takes opportunities to pause and to ruminate, exploring the depths of the words, so that 'heart speaks to heart' in silent communion.

Lectio is another practice with a long history and one that took on new impetus when the Bible began to be translated into the everyday languages of the emerging European nations in the sixteenth century. This development went hand in hand with the new inventions of printing books using movable type and of multiplying images by the processes of woodcut and etching.

To make an etching an artist prepares a metal plate, covering it with an acid-resistant ground, like wax. Then a design is drawn through the protective layer, using an etching needle to expose the metal surface. The plate is then immersed in an acid such as nitric acid for varying lengths of time, depending on the depth of line required. After this the protective ground is removed and the plate is inked, then wiped, so that the ink remains only in the etched grooves. Finally the plate is put in a press in contact with dampened paper, producing an image in reverse of that originally drawn. The artist may decide to vary the effect by further strengthening the etched lines directly on the plate with a burin or other sharp tool. Similarly, the amount of ink used or the way the plate is wiped can vary, especially to darken the effect. It is obvious that the whole process lends itself to the development of great skill and Rembrandt was a master of the art.

Rembrandt's images of Christ

When Rembrandt was a young artist in seventeenth-century Holland, paintings and statues had been removed from Protestant churches. But people still desired to 'see Jesus'. They wanted illustrations in Bibles and prayer books; they wanted pictures of the life of Christ to aid their prayers, to hang on their walls at home. One of Rembrandt's early commissions, in 1634 from the Stadtholder of Amsterdam, was to paint five scenes of the life of Christ. For the rest of his life Rembrandt returned to the Bible for subjects of paintings, drawings and etchings. He produced works of profound beauty and spiritual depth. Rembrandt's images of Christ lead us to the depths of the mystery of the Son of God, the Light of the World. They illuminate Christ's compassionate humanity while at the same time revealing something of Rembrant's own response to the Gospels. By peopling the stories of Christ's life with delicately observed drawings of his own neighbours, many of them Jews, Rembrandt not only shows his compassion, he invites us to do the same. In our praying with these images we can bring the events of the life of Christ into our lives and into the turmoil of today's world. We can allow them to transform us. In this way the insights of one of the greatest of European artists will continue to feed Christian prayer.

Ways to use this book

You can dip into the book at any place, or work through from the beginning, perhaps reading one meditation every day. The order is roughly the story of the life of Christ.

Before you begin, find a quiet place and relax, opening your mind and heart to the presence of God. Choose your meditation and look first at the picture. Let your eye follow the lines of the composition, lines which lead you to recognise what is most important in the event depicted. Then read the Gospel passage slowly, turning back to the picture as you do so, allowing both the visual image and the words to reverberate within you. At any point you could close the book and spend time in silent meditation.

Or go on to read the commentary which will offer you a path into the artist's response to Christ's action as well as to the feelings of the people in the scene and your own thoughts and feelings. If you have a Bible to hand you may wish to follow the references and read more of the Gospel passages that relate to the incident depicted.

Another response is to use the 'words to ponder' like a mantra, a repeated word to help your concentration. Such words can ward off distracting thoughts and deepen your awareness of the message. Or they may simply lead into a peaceful state of resting in the light and spirit of Christ.

This book is not written to convey information, to encourage introspection, or to offer handy hints on how to live a godly life. It is offered as one way to enter into contemplative prayer, not as an escape from the drama of being in the world, but as an entry into the presence of God, who dwells among us in the person of Christ. In this presence, the responses are as various as the persons who pray: adoration, delight, praise; grief or gratitude; the longing for forgiveness; the wordless plea for the needs of all.

When you are ready to conclude your meditation, pray the final prayer. A few of these prayers are contemporary with the etchings. Most take their form from the traditional prayers of Christian worship, to the Father, through the Son, in the power of the Spirit, uniting the individual with all believers.

PART ONE

THE CHILDHOOD OF CHRIST

Rembrandt van RIJN

Dutch 1606-1669

The angel appearing to the shepherds 1634

etching, drypoint and burin

26.2 x 21.7 cm

Felton Bequest, 1933

The Angel Appearing to the Shepherds

In the region of Bethlehem there were shepherds living in the fields, keeping watch over their flock by night. Then an angel of the Lord stood before them, and the glory of the Lord shone around them, and they were terrified.

But the angel said to them, 'Do not be afraid; for see – I am bringing you good news of great joy for all the people: to you is born this day in the city of David a Saviour, who is the Messiah, the Lord.

This will be a sign for you: you will find a child wrapped in bands of cloth and lying in a manger.

And suddenly there was with the angel a multitude of the heavenly host, praising God and saying,

'Glory to God in the highest heaven,
and on earth peace among those whom God favours.'

Luke 2:8–14

This is one of the earliest of Rembrandt's etchings, made when he was 28, the year in which he married Saskia van Ulenburgh. In the same year he received a commission to paint five scenes from the life of Christ for the Stadtholder of Amsterdam. So he would have been reading the Gospel stories of Jesus and experimenting with ways to show the story and the meaning.

This etching is like a prelude to a life of Christ, a dramatic announcement that brings together two worlds: the world of heaven – of light and splendour where crowds of angels praise God – and the world of earth, here shown in darkness, shepherds and animals huddled together in a rocky gorge, shocked into fear by the commanding appearance of the messenger from God.

Rembrandt is already a master at showing light, a theme throughout his etchings, as it is throughout the Gospel stories of Christ, the Light of the World.

Take the time to gaze at the picture. As your eyes become accustomed to the fine detail, more of the scene becomes clear. Is this the artist's intention? We are so used to getting the message in an instant, surrounded as we are by strident images: Look at me! Buy this! Beware! But these etchings were made for meditation. Searching the picture is perhaps a metaphor for the lifetime we can spend pondering the meaning of the angel's message to the world.

Rembrandt did not make an etching of the Annunciation, a subject chosen by so many artists. Instead of showing the intimate moment when the angel Gabriel appeared to tell Mary that she would give birth to a son, the young Rembrandt has given us this Annunciation to the shepherds. It is a characteristically dramatic choice to pitch us into the wonder and mystery of the birth of the Messiah. But we have to work at it.

As you pray, allow your eye to move across the picture between the two worlds. Open yourself to the darkness and to the light. Enter into the feelings of the shepherds. Join with the angels in praising God. Pray in faith and hope for peace on earth.

KEEP WATCH

Loving God, as the darkness that covered the earth gives way to the light of your new creation, lead us out of our fears and confusion to hear the message of the angel. Through our faith in Jesus, may we bring your life to the waiting world.

DO NOT BE AFRAID

JOY AND PEACE

Rembrandt van RIJN

Dutch 1606-1669

The adoration of the shepherds: with the lamp c.1654

etching

10.5 x 13.0 cm

Felton Bequest, 1933

Rembrandt f.

The Adoration of the Shepherds

When the angels had left the shepherds and gone into heaven, the shepherds said to one another, 'Let us go now to Bethlehem and see this thing that has taken place which the Lord has made known to us.'

So they went with haste and found Mary and Joseph, and the child lying in the manger.

When they saw this they made known what had been told them about this child; and all who heard it were amazed at what the shepherds told them.

But Mary treasured all these words and pondered them in her heart.

The shepherds returned, glorifying and praising God for all they had heard and seen, as it had been told them.

Luke 2:15-20

This etching is also referred to as *The Adoration of the Shepherds: with the Lamp* because some versions do not include a lamp. Why is the lamp there? Is it the main source of light in the picture? Once again Rembrandt is seeing something special about light and about Christ as the light for all, the light that shines in the darkness [John1:4-5]. He probably also knew the other references in the Gospels to lamps: If the lamp is put on the lampstand it gives light to the whole house [Matthew 5:14-16]. And the story of the bridesmaids who made sure they had oil in their lamps to welcome the bridegroom [Matthew 25:1-3].

The stable scene is intimate, almost cosy, as the wondering shepherds lean down towards the mother and child. The shepherds have passed on the angel's message about the birth of a Saviour. Now they feast their eyes on the child. One of them is shielding his eyes from the brightness of the light that seems to come from the child even more than from the lamp.

Joseph sits on an upturned barrow. He opens his hands and looks across to the shepherds as if to say, 'See!' But Mary is absorbed. Her right hand holds her cloak, encircling the close-wrapped baby but the pose of her head is thoughtful, treasuring the shepherd's message, wondering what it could mean.

The massive heads of the oxen seem to stoop in reverence. Legend has it that the animals' breath warmed the little family who could find no other shelter in Bethlehem.

Rembrandt made this etching twenty years after *The Angel Appearing to the Shepherds.* There is not the same drama of stark contrasts. The whole scene is calm and thoughtful. Now the great mystery of God among us is presented in the simplicity of home and family, of shelter, of relationship and love. The artist's family life was chaotic. For most of us the same is true. And for how many people throughout the world does life offer only moments of haven, snatched from strife and wandering? As it did in Rembrandt's time of civil and religious wars.

Let your eyes move around the lamplit circle so that you too can ponder all these things in your heart. Or you may prefer to focus on the lamp. Or on the mysterious shining space that Rembrandt seems to place in nearly all of his etched scenes. What is this space for you? Where does it take you as you enter your time of silent prayer?

THEY FOUND THE CHILD

Welcome all wonders in one sight,
Eternity shut in a span,
Summer in winter, day in night,
Heaven in earth, and God in man!
Great little one! whose all-embracing birth
Lifts earth to heaven, stoops heaven to earth.

RICHARD CRASHAW 1613-49

THEY RETURNED PRAISING GOD

MARY TREASURED ALL THESE WORDS

Rembrandt van RIJN
Dutch 1606–1669
The flight into Egypt: a night piece 1651
etching, drypoint and burin
12.8 x 11.0 cm
Felton Bequest, 1933

Rembrandt van RIJN
Dutch 1606-1669
The flight into Egypt: the Holy Family crossing a brook 1654
etching and drypoint
9.4 x 14.4 cm
Felton Bequest, 1923

The Flight into Egypt

Now after the wise men had left Bethlehem, an angel of the Lord appeared to Joseph in a dream and said, 'Get up, take the child and his mother, and flee to Egypt, and remain there until I tell you; for Herod is about to search for the child, to destroy him.'

Then Joseph got up, took the child and his mother by night, and went to Egypt, and remained there until the death of Herod. This was to fulfil what had been spoken by the Lord through the prophet, 'Out of Egypt I have called my son'.

Matthew 2:13-15

Rembrandt made several etchings of *The Flight into Egypt*. They bring together his interest in landscape, in the closeness of people and animals, in the struggle to find a way out of dangerous darkness into the daylight of peace and security. Like the Jews in the time of Christ, the Dutch in Rembrandt's time were familiar with the plight of innocent people finding themselves refugees in the midst of warring factions.

Look first at the night scene. Take time to search the darkness. If you can, as your eye searches the dark picture, allow your mind to search into the dark places of experience. Like Joseph you have a lamp of faith to guide you.

Or perhaps you feel impelled to set aside thought and to rest your mind, in the darkness that is the mystery of God.

When you are ready, return again to the picture and see the patient face of Joseph as he looks ahead into the darkness, one hand firmly holding the lamp, the other leading the donkey. The donkey too looks patient, his head close to Joseph's side, ears pricked forward, alert to the task of carrying safely a precious burden. The light just touches Mary's head but as you continue to gaze, the shape of the donkey and the suggestion of the child's head begin to emerge.

The Gospel story does not give any details about how the family travelled and artists have offered many settings. Rembrandt's is simple and dramatic. This is a poor family, travelling without a retinue, trusting themselves to the strength of a humble animal. Today they might be refugees in a leaky boat, or hitching a ride in the back of a truck.

Three years later Rembrandt made another etching of *The Flight into Egypt*. This shows the little family crossing a brook. There is more light and you can see the wildness of the terrain. The donkey is less sure about the water; his ears are flattened back and Joseph's hand holds the bridle firmly. Joseph is lunging forward, his stick probing the bed of the stream. This is a dangerous part of the journey. But Mary sits calmly, cuddling the baby, her head tilted, her gaze reflective. Her free hand grips the donkey's rug, bracing herself against the animal's lurching steps. Is she conscious of present pain? Or thinking of what is to come, of the life journey that she and her son will make? In Rembrandt's scene she is a firm pyramid, a place of rest and hope in the midst of turmoil.

THEY WENT BY NIGHT

Ever loving and faithful God,
you sent your son to be our light.
Through the prayers of Mary and Joseph,
guide us on our journey as we too carry
the Christ child into the world.

I CALLED MY SON

REMAIN THERE UNTIL I TELL YOU

Rembrandt van RIJN
Dutch 1606-1669
Christ seated, disputing with the doctors 1654
etching
9.5 x 14.4 cm
Felton Bequest, 1923

Rembrandt f. 1654

Christ Disputing with the Doctors

Every year Jesus' parents went up to Jerusalem for the festival of the Passover. And when Jesus was twelve years old, they went up as usual for the festival. When the festival was ended and they started to return, the boy Jesus stayed behind in Jerusalem, but his parents did not know it.

Assuming that he was in the group of travellers, they went a day's journey. Then they started to look for him among their relatives and friends. When they did not find him, they returned to Jerusalem to search for him.

After three days they found him in the temple, sitting among the teachers, listening to them and asking them questions. And all who heard him were amazed at his understanding and his answers.

Luke 2:41-47

Rembrandt set many scenes of the life of Christ in poor and simple surroundings, like the first three etchings in this book. But now there is a change. The setting is the city of Jerusalem, in the temple itself, the heart of the power, wisdom and tradition of the Jewish religion. Although the architecture is only loosely sketched in, it is massive and the grouping of the figures is monumental, static and all male. But this is not a scene of confrontation. It is more subtle than that.

Jesus and his parents have come as good Jews in obedience to the custom that required a pilgrimage to the holy city. They make their offering and set out for home. Jesus remains behind for another whole day among the learned teachers. He listens but he also asks questions and the teachers are amazed at his answers. Here is the mystery of a new revelation that grows out of an ancient tradition. A new voice that would eventually bring down upon itself the wrath of the whole establishment.

Rembrandt has arranged the figures in this etching to lead the eye to the young Jesus. He does this especially by the diagonal groupings on the right, and by the contrasts between the boy and the older men. Look at each man in relation to Jesus. Look at the man with his back turned, the man hovering over Jesus, the bulky man seated beside him, the tall one standing in the centre.

Perhaps the diversity of the group is emphasised to highlight the diversity of the questions they put to Jesus. Look at the feet. (Jesus is the only one with bare feet.) Look at the hands; above all look at the faces, the listening expressions. Imagine what this group are like when they argue with each other. But now all are silent, listening to a child. Rembrandt shows himself a master of 'drawing' speech as he creates a space and a silence around the boy. This etching is called *Christ Disputing with the Doctors* but it does not look like a dispute. The roles are reversed and it looks like a teacher with thoughtful pupils.

For the first time in the Gospels, Jesus speaks! In the presence of this voice my voice is still, my doubts silenced, my learning put aside. In the presence of the Word of God, like the teachers in the temple, I am stilled into astonishment and awe. This is a moment to hold, to close the book, and hear what Jesus is saying to me.

THEY WENT UP TO JERUSALEM

Blessed Jesus, at your word
we are gathered all to hear you;
let our minds and hearts be stirred
now to seek to love and fear you;
by your gospel pure and holy
teach us, Lord, to love you solely.

TOBIAS CLAUSNITZNER, 1619-84

THEY SEARCHED FOR HIM

ALL WERE AMAZED

Rembrandt van RIJN
Dutch 1606-1669
Christ between his parents, returning from the temple 1654
etching and drypoint
9.4 x 14.4 cm
Purchased through The Art Foundation of Victoria with the assistance of Miss Flora McDonald and Mrs Ethel Elizabeth Ogilvy Lumsden, Founder Benefactors, 1987

Rembrandt f. 1654

Christ between his Parents Returning from Jerusalem

When his parents saw Jesus [in the temple] they were astonished; and his mother said to him, 'Child, why have you treated us like this? Look, your father and I have been searching for you in great anxiety.'

He said to them, 'Why were you searching for me? Did you not know that I must be in my Father's house?' But they did not understand what he said to them.

Then Jesus went down with Mary and Joseph and came to Nazareth and was obedient to them.

His mother treasured all these things in her heart.

And Jesus increased in wisdom and in years and in divine and human favour.

Luke 2:48-52

Rembrandt's first two children died in infancy. His son Titus was the only child to survive into adulthood. In 1654, when Rembrandt made this etching, Titus was thirteen years old. Rembrandt's wife, Saskia, had died within a year of Titus' birth. Also by 1654 Rembrandt was deeply in debt as well as in trouble with the authorities because Hendrickje Stoffels, who lived with them, was not his wife. It is against this background that we can contemplate his picture of Christ and his parents returning home from Jerusalem.

They are walking purposefully up a rising slope, ahead of the crowd of travellers who linger in the in the valley below. The dog sets the pace. Mary and Joseph have just been through the harrowing experience of losing Jesus, so they are holding on to him tightly. Or rather Joseph's big hand is firmly gripping that of his son. Jesus stretches out his right hand to clasp the open hand of his mother, as if to reassure her of his presence.

Joseph's strong face is calm and thoughtful. Mary leans across to her son as if she is listening to what Jesus has just said. He is half turned to Mary but his head is thrown back and he looks upward in a striking pose that makes him the centre of the picture.

Is he still thinking of his experience in the temple? Is he wondering about the two homes, his foster father's house in Nazareth to which they are returning, and his heavenly father's house signified by the temple in Jerusalem? Jesus' whole human life will be a journey to Jerusalem; as we now know, a journey to a savage death. Yet here, he is still a child. He does not know where his fidelity to his heavenly father's message of love will take him. Does he begin to suspect? Perhaps Rembrandt is giving us a hint by placing in Mary's hand a loaf of bread. . .

This etching is another example of Rembrandt's genius at catching the moment of enlightenment on a journey; enlightenment for Jesus, for Mary and Joseph, surely for Rembrandt himself, and for us. Take time to trace the road through the rocky landscape. Allow the wonderful energy of this journeying family to well up within you.

Hold this moment of revelation. Hold in your heart: your life, your loves, your family, your journey. Close the book and allow God to speak to you.

JESUS WENT HOME WITH THEM

Lord make me your dwelling.
May my heart and spirit always be ready to receive you.
May you find my house swept,
my table spread and my lamp ready
to be lit by your presence.

WHY TREAT US LIKE THIS?

JESUS INCREASED IN WISDOM

PART TWO

THE MESSAGE OF LOVE

Rembrandt van RIJN

Dutch 1606-1669

Christ preaching (La petite tombe) c.1652

etching, drypoint and burin

15.5 x 20.7 cm

Felton Bequest, 1933

Christ Preaching

Jesus said, 'I thank you, Father, Lord of heaven and of earth, because you have hidden these things from the wise and the intelligent and have revealed them to infants. Yes, Father, for such was your gracious will. All things have been handed over to me by my Father; and no-one knows the Son except the Father; and no-one knows the Father except the Son and anyone to whom the Son chooses to reveal him.

Come to me all you that are weary and carrying heavy burdens, and I will give you rest. Take my yoke upon you, and learn from me; for I am gentle and humble in heart and you will find rest for your souls. For my yoke is easy and my burden is light.

Matthew 11:25-30

In Matthew's Gospel Jesus is usually preaching to the crowds in the countryside, on a mountain, or by the sea. But Rembrandt set many scenes in the closed-in spaces of a town, perhaps to make them more relevant to the lives of the townspeople who would buy the etchings. And he used as models people who lived around him. Indeed the listeners in this famous etching are so intimately observed that they must have been drawn from life.

Imagine that this crowd are a group of people that you know. Take the time to linger over each one. Notice the way the light falls lovingly on a cheek, a shoulder, a kerchief, a bald head, a beard, a clenched fist, a pair of bare heels. Only Jesus and the child are barefoot. Is there a message here about innocence? Is there a message in the light itself? It seems to caress each individual, knowingly, loving each one with Christ's love.

Is there a space in this little circle for you? Is there a light for you? Where does the light come from?

We do not know which of Christ's words Rembrandt had in mind here but the expressions suggest that they were consoling words. Jesus stands with hands upraised in the ancient gesture of prayer, of blessing, of self-giving. He looks lovingly on the people gathered around him. His eyes seem especially directed to the woman and the children sitting at his feet. This etching has been called a perfect illustration of a voice. Every listener is wrapt in attention, wondering, trusting, surprised, thoughtful, perhaps saying, 'Can it really be so? What does this mean for me?'

Perhaps your eye is drawn back, beyond the figure of Jesus, to the courtyard with its suggestions of doorways, roofs, inner rooms. Does your prayer take you into an inner room, there to treasure the words of Jesus?

Or do you prefer to seat yourself among the crowd as you let Jesus speak to you. What might his words mean in your life?

This picture could be a starting point for many meditations on the words of Jesus. You could imagine this scene as you read the Sermon on the Mount [Matthew chapter 5] or the passage where Jesus teaches the disciples to pray. [Matthew chapter 6]. Listen to that voice as you move into your time of silent prayer.

YOU WHO
ARE WEARY
COME
TO ME

Loving God, our father and our mother,
look on the heart of Christ
filled with love for us.
Because of his love, draw us
into the circle of your love.
Help us to recognise him in those around us.

TAKE MY
YOKE
UPON YOU

YOU WILL
FIND
REST

Rembrandt van RIJN
Dutch 1606-1669
The return of the prodigal son 1636
etching
15.6 x 13.6 cm
Felton Bequest, 1933

Rembrandt f 1636
91

The Return of the Prodigal Son

Then Jesus said, 'There was a man who had two sons. The younger of them said to his father, "Father, give me the share of the property that will belong to me." So he divided his property between them. A few days later the younger son gathered all he had and travelled to a distant country, and there he squandered his property in dissolute living. When he had spent everything, a severe famine took place throughout that country, and he began to be in need. So he went and hired himself out to one of the citizens of that country, who sent him to his fields to feed his pigs. He would gladly have filled himself with the pods that the pigs were eating; and no one gave him anything. But when he came to himself he said, "How many of my father's hired hands have bread enough and to spare, but here I am dying of hunger. I will get up and go to my father, and I will say to him, "Father, I have sinned against heaven and before you; I am no longer worthy to be called your son; treat me like one of your hired hands."

So he set off and went to his father. But while he was still far off, his father saw him and was filled with compassion; he ran and put his arms around him and kissed him. Then the son said to the father, "Father, I have sinned against heaven and before you; I am no longer worthy to be called your son."

But the father said to his slaves, "Quickly bring out a robe – the best one – and put it on him; put a ring on his finger and sandals on his feet and get the fatted calf and kill it, and let us eat and celebrate; for this son of mine was dead and is alive again; he was lost and is found!" And they began to celebrate.'

LUKE 15:11-25

Rembrandt made this etching in 1636. He was only thirty years old but already a famous portrait painter and making the most of his new position. Did he begin to recognise that perhaps his path might follow that of the feckless son in the gospel story?

Around this time, Rembrandt's first child, a son Rombertus, was born and died. Now he knows the joy and grief of fatherhood. What thoughts and feelings would he bring to his depiction of Jesus' story about the loving father who welcomes home the son who went away!

This is a threshold scene, a moment of encounter. The space at the left hints at the vast distance of the rough world, the journey that the son has travelled. His thrown-down stick is delicately balanced on the upper step, pointing back the way he has come. But the son has cast away the stick, climbed the steps and fallen to his knees. On the right the steps lead up and into the house where the servants are waiting with the robe and the ring. But everything in the picture leads the eye to the central circle as the father's body curves down to embrace the son. The father's beard mingles with the tangled hair of the gaunt and ragged son. The son's head rests in the cradling security of the father's breast. The father is not looking at the son's clasped hands or hearing the stumbling voice that stammers the prepared appeal. The father's whole body is expressive of acceptance and forgiveness.

Jesus tells this story to show us something about God. We can think of God as like a loving father and of ourselves as children dwelling in his household. True loving must be between equals and God will not force us. We are left free to return love for love. God does not want just lip-service. The father will not for a moment allow the son to be a servant.

The son has returned to his father's house. He has returned to the love and friendship that he rejected when he took his inheritance in a futile attempt to find a freedom elsewhere. But money did not bring freedom and he realised at last that his true riches lay in the love that surrounded him at home. It is characteristic of the father that forgiveness was instantaneous.

The father's arms embrace all who have chosen to leave home, to move outside the circle of friendship, to experience the coldness of a world that values only possessions and position. When we choose to return, he has no need to punish us. We have punished ourselves enough.

Above the father's head, a watcher (perhaps the other son) opens a window and looks down. Place yourself with the watcher and look down on this moment of reconciliation and homecoming. Or enter into the circle of the loving embrace that welcomes you home whenever you turn and open yourself to God's love.

I WILL GO TO MY FATHER

Be mindful of your mercy, O Lord,
and your steadfast love,
for they have been from of old.
Do not remember the sins of my youth
or my transgressions;
according to your steadfast love remember me
for your goodness' sake, O Lord!

Psalm 25:6-7

FATHER, I HAVE SINNED

HE PUT HIS ARMS AROUND HIM

Rembrandt van RIJN
Dutch 1606-1669
Christ with the sick around him, receiving little children
(The Hundred Guilder Print) c.1649
etching, drypoint and burin
28.1 x 39.4 cm
Purchased 1891

Christ with the Sick around Him, Receiving Little Children

JESUS LEFT GALILEE and went to the region of Judea beyond the Jordan. Large crowds followed him, and he cured them there.

MATTHEW 19:1-2

This is one of the most famous of all Rembrandt's etchings, dated around 1649 though he probably worked on it for ten years or more.

Unlike most of the other etchings this one does not so much show one event as a distillation of Christ's whole mission of healing and preaching. Chapter 19 of Matthew's Gospel is suggested as the main source but the picture shows more than that. There are echoes of many Gospel passages. It is as if Jesus stands, a pivotal point, and around him the shifting crowd slowly moves, grouping and regrouping as one incident after another comes into focus. It is a bit like the posters one sometimes sees, of a book or a film, where all the characters are shown together in a way they never were in the story. A picture like this makes a starting point for many meditations – no doubt one of the artist's intentions.

I am the light of the world. Whoever follows me will never walk in darkness but will have the light of life.

JOHN 8:12

The movement from dark to light across the picture, the skillful composition with the sick emerging from the darkness on the right, and above all the central presence of Christ himself, radiating light, make this one picture a profound experience of encounter with Jesus, one to which we can return time and again - just as people did who bought prints of it in Rembrandt's time.

Seek the face of Christ! Look for him where he is to be found. What does faith in Christ mean for me? What is my journey from darkness to light? Is mine the shadow of pleading hands that falls across his robe?

Then little children were brought to Jesus in order that he might lay his hands on them and pray. The disciples spoke sternly to those who brought them; but Jesus said, 'Let the little children come to me, and do not stop them; for it is to such as these that the kingdom of heaven belongs.' And he laid his hands on them and went on his way.

MATTHEW 19: 13-15

Look at the picture again. Christ's right hand reaches out to the strong young woman who steps up to him presenting her child. Her whole pose is energetic; her workday skirts are tucked up and her feet placed firmly. You can sense the muscles in her back. She is the bearer and nurturer of her child. She brings her child, her life, herself to Jesus.

Like her I come to Jesus. Am I here the mother offering creativity and maturity? Or the child whose potential is offered in hope?
Perhaps this is the place to pause, holding the moment of offering...

The figure of the man at Jesus right is warning the woman off, protesting to Jesus. The disciples have their own ideas of Jesus' mission and these do not include women and children! On the far left another group of men sit around a table arguing, not looking at Jesus. These may be the Pharisees, still discussing the legality of divorce [Matthew 19:3-12]. Rembrandt has moved them into the background. Jesus is beckoning and blessing the women and children.

Look at the other woman who carries a baby in her arms. She is hesitant but hopeful, dragged forward by the toddler. The child has been distracted from his game with the dog and is eager to move to Jesus. The dog is waiting to continue the game.

'Unless you change and become like children, you will never enter the kingdom of heaven.'

MATTHEW 18: 3

Between the two women is another figure, neither immersed in the men's talk nor moving, like the women, to Jesus. He sits, chin in hand, pondering. This figure is interpreted as the rich young man mentioned in Matthew 19:16-22.

Then a young man came to Jesus and said, 'Teacher, what good deed must I do to have eternal life?' And Jesus said to him, 'Why do you ask me about what is good? There is only one who is good. If you wish to enter into eternal life, keep the commandments.'

The young man said to him, 'Which ones?' Jesus said, 'You shall not murder. You shall not commit adultery; You shall not steal; You shall not bear false witness; Honour your father and your mother; also, You shall love your neighbour as yourself.'

The young man said to him , 'I have kept all these; what do I still lack?' Jesus said to him, 'If you wish to be perfect, go sell your possessions, and give the money to the poor, and you will have treasure in heaven; then come follow me.'

When the young man heard this word, he went away grieving, for he had many possessions.

The sadness, the uncertainty, of this young man as he sits in his fine clothes, reflecting on Jesus' words, sums up the human longing for perfection, the longing for the treasure that alone will satisfy those who 'seek the face of God'. Rembrandt by this time was in debt, plagued by creditors. Eight years later, he was to suffer the loss of all his possessions when he was declared bankrupt. All his goods, including precious collections of paintings and etchings were sold off to pay creditors. Did he think back to the young man he had drawn in this etching? Is this why he had to buy back a print, to keep the words of Jesus in mind? (This etching is known as *The Hundred Guilder Print,* the price Rembrandt had to pay to get it back.)

With whom do I identify? What do I cling to? What am I afraid of losing? Can I set aside my fears and follow Jesus with the eagerness of the child in this picture? Or do I still sit uncertain, with the rich young man?

'Truly I tell you, it will be hard for a rich person to enter the kingdom of heaven. Again, I tell you, it is easier for a camel to go through the eye of a needle than for someone who is rich to enter the kingdom of God'.

When the disciples heard this, they were greatly astounded and said, 'Who then can be saved?' But Jesus looked at them and said, 'For mortals it is impossible, but for God all things are possible.' Then Peter said in reply, 'Look, we have left everything and followed you. What then will we have?'

Jesus said to them, 'Truly I tell you, at the renewal of all things, when the Son of Man is seated on the throne of his glory, you who have followed me will also sit on twelve thrones, judging the twelve tribes of Israel. And everyone who has left houses or brothers or sisters or father or mother or children or fields, for my name's sake, will receive a hundredfold, and will inherit eternal life. But many who are first will be last, and the last will be first.

MATTHEW 19:23-30

Those closest to Jesus are the poor and the sick. The rich man is barely visible, standing in the darkness on the right of the picture, in his hat and fine clothes, camel and attendant nearby – an ironic touch? Moving out of the shadows into the light that surrounds Jesus comes the widow, her hands gesturing to the dead body of her son [perhaps Luke 7:11-16]. She asks for life. A blind man is led forward, leaning on his stick. He asks to see. Another woman, too sick to rise, lifts one hand to touch the hem of Jesus' robe [Mark:5:25-29]. Two more kneel, pleading with clasped hands, eyes fixed on Jesus.

I fix my eyes on Jesus and pray for the healing of my mind and body and soul.

Rembrandt used as models the people who lived around him, many of them Jews. Did the artist see Christ among them as he worked and reworked this etching, lightening and darkening, altering the groupings, bringing one figure forward, then another? Did his own faith deepen as he recognised Christ, the one who heals, the one who welcomes the poor and the sick? The one for whom it is worth leaving all; the one who takes into his loving embrace all human loss.

Can I live with this picture day by day, as generations of believers have done before?

LET THE CHILDREN COME

O Jesus, light of all below,
fount of life and fire,
surpassing all the joys we know,
and all we can desire.
Abide with us and let thy light
shine, Lord, on every heart,
dispel the darkness of our night
and joy to all impart.

BERNARD OF CLAIRVAUX, 1091–1153

SELL ALL AND GIVE

LORD THAT I MAY SEE

Rembrandt van RIJN

Dutch 1606-1669

Christ and the woman of Samaria: among ruins 1634

etching

12.3 x 10.8 cm

Felton Bequest, 1958

Rembrandt. f. 1634

Christ and the Woman of Samaria

Jesus came to a Samaritan city called Sychar, near the plot of ground that Jacob had given to his son Joseph. Jacob's well was there, and Jesus, tired out by his journey, was sitting by the well. It was about noon.

A Samaritan woman came to draw water, and Jesus said to her, 'Give me a drink.' (His disciples had gone to the city to buy food.) The Samaritan woman said to him, 'How is it that you, a Jew, ask a drink of me, a woman of Samaria?' (Jews do not share things in common with Samaritans.)

Jesus answered her, 'If you knew who it is that is saying to you, "Give me a drink", you would have asked him, and he would have given you living water.'

The woman said to him, 'Sir, you have no bucket, and the well is deep. Where do you get that living water? Are you greater than our ancestor Jacob, who gave us the well, and with his sons and his flocks drank from it?'

Jesus said to her, 'Everyone who drinks of this water will be thirsty again, but those who drink of the water that I will give them will never thirst again. The water that I will give will become in them a spring of water gushing up to eternal life.'

The woman said to him, 'Sir, give me this water, so that I may never be thirsty or have to keep coming here to draw water.'

JOHN 4:5-15

Rembrandt made this etching in 1634, the year of his marriage to Saskia, a marriage that was not welcomed by the bride's family. But love crosses boundaries and this story is about how, in Jesus, the love of God breaks through the boundaries set up by custom and convention.

Jesus was tired out by his journey. Is this a reference to his journey to Jerusalem, the last journey of his life? It was noon; in the heat of the day he rested while his disciples went to buy food. Unusually, for women would come for water early in the day, one woman approaches. Seeing a Jewish man by the well, she must have expected rejection.

The Jews did not associate with the Samaritans. There were ancient antagonisms between them. Nor would a man engage publicly in conversation with a woman. (No wonder that when Jesus' disciples returned they were astonished to find him talking to a Samaritan woman.) Jesus opens the conversation abruptly, 'Give me a drink.'

How does the artist signal this encounter across boundaries? Most obvious is the contrast between the dark ruined archway behind Jesus, perhaps the temple whose destruction he predicted, and the opening out to distant skies behind the woman. And the vertical of the well-head post and chain divides the two people even as their hands and glances move towards each other.

Let your eye move down from the crumbling wall to the figure of Jesus, balanced on the edge of the well, awkward but eager, one foot poised in the air as he leans across the dark circle towards the woman. This conversation is food and drink to him.

See how the woman stands firm, braced confidently against the waist-high parapet, as she replies, 'Sir you have no bucket!' Yet has she begun to realise that this is no ordinary encounter? Her head is not flung back as you might expect, but tilted and turning to the light as if in wonder.

What can the stranger mean? Her daily journey to the well has brought home to the woman the relentlessness of human thirst, quenched only to rage again. Jesus uses this familiar awareness to shift her thinking. Now water becomes a symbol of a divine, life-giving gift, forever welling up; a spring of water gushing eternal life.

God's gift of love is not confined to the privileged but offered to all, across all boundaries. In many of his etchings of the life of Christ, Rembrandt seems to recognise this truth. He sets the scenes in the midst of everyday life, lovingly drawing each figure, touching them with light, the way God's love touches them.

Let your eyes move again between Jesus and the woman. Hear the words of Jesus. Open yourself to the hope of living water, rising up in the deep well of the heart, available to all who have faith in Jesus Christ, 'truly the saviour of the world'.

THE WELL IS DEEP

Ever faithful and loving God,
at the very dawn of creation
your spirit breathed on the waters
making them a wellspring of holiness.
Create in me a pure heart and fill me
with the spirit of your son, Jesus Christ.

GIVE ME THIS WATER

NEVER THIRST AGAIN

Rembrandt van RIJN

Dutch 1606-1669

The raising of Lazarus: the larger plate c.1632

etching and burin

36.3 x 25.8 cm

Felton Bequest, 1962

The Raising of Lazarus

Then Jesus, greatly disturbed, came to the tomb. It was a cave, and a stone was lying against it. Jesus said, 'Take away the stone.' Martha, the sister of the dead man, said to Jesus, 'Lord, already there is a stench because he has been dead four days.' Jesus said to her, 'Did I not tell you that if you believed, you would see the glory of God?'

So they took away the stone. And Jesus looked upward and said, 'Father, I thank you for having heard me. I knew that you always hear me, but I have said this for the sake of the crowd standing here, so that they may believe that you sent me.' When he had said this, he cried with a loud voice, 'Lazarus, come out!'

The dead man came out, his hands and feet bound with strips of cloth, and his face wrapped in a cloth. Jesus said, 'Unbind him, and let him go.' Many of the Jews who had come with Mary and had seen what Jesus did, believed in him.

John 11:38-45

This is the earliest etching in this collection, made when Rembrandt was 26. He had recently moved to Amsterdam and was making his name as a portrait painter. The extreme dramatic contrasts of this picture are more characteristic of his youthful years than the stripped down, simplified approach of some of his later etchings.

Of course the event, on any consideration, is dramatic. And it was to have dramatic consequences for Christ as well as for the women whose brother Lazarus was returned to life.

In Rembrandt's scene Christ dominates; his power and assurance are apparent in every line even though his face is turned away from us. His stillness of body and confidently upraised hand is in contrast to the twisted bodies, agitated faces, stunned looks of the bystanders, though it is echoed in the calm face and still pose of Lazarus lying in the grave. The artist has chosen to show the awesome moment when the dead man begins to come to life. His mouth opens, gasping for a first breath. The heavy-lidded eyes still resist the light. Truly he is being born again.

Look at the two women, the sisters Mary and Martha. One is almost toppling into the grave in her amazement while the other, on the right, is a wonderful little portrait of awakening hope and delight.

Jesus told Martha that she would see the glory of God and Rembrandt suggests this glory in cascades of light. Jesus' friends still do not recognise in him the gift of God, the loving gift of eternal life beyond human imagining. As Jesus raises his hand and calls Lazarus to life can we catch the mighty voice of the Word of God calling all things into being?

Here, we are at the heart of our own vocation, our own calling into life. In our times of silent prayer we listen for that voice, quiet now, not forcing us, but always waiting for our love. Can we respond, 'Lord I believe', as did many who saw the miracle?

But there were also stirrings of envy among the religious leaders who saw their position threatened and began to plot against Jesus. 'From that day on they planned to put him to death.' [John 11:53]

I AM THE RESURRECTION AND THE LIFE

Ever-loving God,
your Word, Jesus Christ,
overcame death and
brought Lazarus to life.
Fill us with faith in your love,
and raise us also to new life
in the name of Jesus.

LAZARUS COME OUT

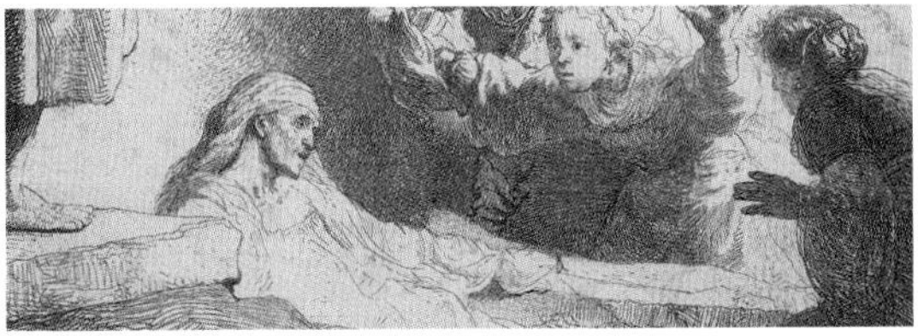

UNBIND HIM AND LET HIM GO

PART THREE

LOVE GREATER THAN DEATH

Rembrandt van RIJN

Dutch 1606-1669

Christ presented to the people: large oblong plate 1655

drypoint

35.9 x 45.5 cm

Felton Bequest, 1940

Christ Presented to the People

Now at the festival the governor was accustomed to release a prisoner for the crowd, anyone whom they wanted. At that time they had a notorious prisoner, called Barabbas. So after they had gathered, Pilate said to them, 'Whom do you want me to release for you, Barabbas or Jesus who is called the Messiah?' For he realised that it was out of jealousy that they had handed him over.

While Pilate was sitting on the judgement seat, his wife sent word to him, 'Have nothing to do with that innocent man, for today I have suffered a great deal because of a dream about him.'

Now the chief priests and elders persuaded the crowds to ask for Barabbas and to have Jesus killed.

Matthew 27:15-20

Rembrandt worked over this scene for many years, coming back to it at different times and altering the emphasis quite dramatically. The picture shows Jesus coming into confrontation with the Law. Rembrandt more than once found himself in a similar position, which may account for his preoccupation with this Gospel passage. This print of the 1655 version shows the moment when Pilate presents Jesus to the people, inviting them to ask for his release.

Pilate and Jesus stand on an elevated platform in front of a municipal building of Rembrandt's time. This is a common 'place of justice', as the carved statues in the upper niches indicate. (They show on the left, Justice, blind, with scales; and on the right Fortitude.) Jesus appears, exposed to public gaze, almost naked, his hands bound, his pose and expression a mixture of resignation and apprehension. Pilate, by contrast wears elaborate robes and a high turban.

The crowd have scarcely noticed either of them yet. Pilate is just beginning his appeal. In a few more moments the scene will break into dramatic action. The elders, hoping to sway the crowd, are moving down the steps at the right. A few in the crowd, perhaps the followers of Jesus, raise their arms to point. In an upper window on the left, Pilate's wife has just sent her message about that 'innocent man'. A servant to the left of the platform stands waiting with the jug of water and the basin in which, after the crowds have screamed for the release of the robber Barabbas, Pilate will 'wash his hands' of Jesus' fate. As with so many of Rembrandt's etchings, the bystanders offer a point of identification for the prayerful viewer.

I place myself among them, ready to watch and wait... Have I ever found myself in such a situation as the people in the crowd? At the least expected time I may be pitched into a moment of choice. Friends, enemies, the requirements of law, my compassion for suffering, all make conflicting appeals. How do I decide? How did I decide? In such moments the action of God's grace can become apparent – or be veiled.

Or do I want to identify myself with the barefoot and innocent Christ, here publicly reduced to the position of a common criminal? Can I enter into my experiences of failure and shame and be open to healing love? Can I enter into the anguish of all who are unjustly accused, and pray for mercy and compassion? In later years Rembrandt reworked this etching, removing the crowd altogether, so that, below the platform, there yawned the cave-like entrance of a dark prison - the gates of death that Christ would open through his loving acceptance of death upon a cross.

WHOM DO YOU WANT?

Jesus, in your face we see our own,
gazing in fear at what is to come.
Give to us, and to all who are bound,
the courage to take your leap
of faith and love.

BARABBAS OR JESUS?

THEY HANDED HIM OVER

Rembrandt van RIJN
Dutch 1606-1669
Christ crucified between two thieves: large oblong plate
(The three crosses) c.1660
drypoint and burin
38.6 x 45.3 cm
Felton Bequest, 1949

Christ Crucified between Two Thieves

From noon on, darkness came over the whole land until three in the afternoon. And about three o'clock Jesus cried with a loud voice, 'Eli, Eli, lema sabachthani?' that is, 'My God, my God, why have you forsaken me?'
When some of the bystanders heard it they said, 'This man is calling for Elijah.' At once one of them ran and got a sponge, filled it with sour wine, put it on a stick and gave it to him to drink.
But others said, 'Wait, let us see whether Elijah will come to save him.'
Then Jesus cried again with a loud voice and breathed his last.

At that moment the curtain of the temple was torn in two from top to bottom. The earth shook, and the rocks were split. The tombs were opened, and the bodies of many saints who had fallen asleep were raised. After his resurrection they came out of the tombs and entered the holy city and appeared to many.

Now when the centurion and those with him who were keeping watch over Jesus, saw the earthquake and what had taken place, they were terrified and said, 'Truly this man was God's Son.'

Matthew 27:45-54

Earlier etchings of Christ crucified show more details of the Gospel story of the death of Jesus. In them one can see clearly the two thieves, the soldiers, the friends of Jesus. All the figures are strongly expressive of emotions and a blaze of heavenly light shines down as Jesus offers his spirit to God. But Rembrandt went on working on this great depiction of the death of Jesus, simplifying and darkening by rescoring the copper plate until, around 1660, he produced the version shown here.

The account of the passion of Christ in Matthew's Gospel best fits this scene with its sense of universal cataclysm overwhelming the personal sorrows of the participants.

The crucified Christ still dominates, but now we hear his desolate imploring cry as he gazes up into the gloom. The deep scoring lines of the etching process still indicate the accepting light from above but the foreground figures can scarcely be made out.

To the left a turbaned horseman, perhaps the symbol of the worldly power that brought Christ to his death, sits erect, while another soldier raises a sword in a gesture frustrated or triumphant? Further left, a soldier tries to hold the head of a horse that rears up in fear. The centurion proclaiming his faith in Christ kneels at the foot of the cross, his head bowed. To the right of the picture, the apostle John stretches out his arms in a gesture of resignation. At Jesus' feet Mary Magdalene clasps the wood of the cross, while Mary the mother of Jesus swoons away into the darkness. It is as if the artist is moving ever closer to experiencing – in his work and in his life – the full power of the moment when Christ, overwhelmed by suffering, offers his life to God and dies.

The contemplation of this moment of the death of Jesus is at the heart of all Christian prayer and life. All voices are silenced; all emotions purged.
How do you respond to this scene? Where do you place yourself?
Can you accompany the artist, and the group around the three crosses, on this journey ever deeper into the truth of your life? Do you fear the darkness may overwhelm you?

Or do you dare, with the centurion, to proclaim that this is truly the Son of God? To believe that the moment, when Jesus gives back to the Father the gift of a loving life, is also the moment of resurrection? You close the book and let the darkness fall.

DARKNESS OVER THE WHOLE LAND

That which is Christ-like within us
shall be crucified.
It shall suffer and be broken.
And that which is Christ-like within us
shall rise up.
It shall love and create.

MICHAEL LEUNIG

JESUS BREATHED HIS LAST

TRULY THIS MAN WAS GOD'S SON

Rembrandt van RIJN

Dutch 1606-1669

The descent from the cross: by torchlight 1654

etching and drypoint

20.8 x 16.1 cm

Felton Bequest, 1933

The Descent from the Cross

After these things, Joseph of Arimathea, who was a disciple of Jesus, though a secret one because of his fear of the Jews, asked Pilate to let him take away the body of Jesus. Pilate gave him permission and he came and removed the body.

Nicodemus, who had at first come to Jesus by night, also came, bringing a mixture of myrrh and aloes, weighing about a hundred pounds. They took the body of Jesus and wrapped it with the spices in linen cloths, according to the custom of the Jews.

John 19:38-40

For hundreds of years artists had painted the complicated manouevres of taking down a dead body from a high cross. Many seized the opportunity to demonstrate how well they could depict the human body, showing the naked Christ gracefully cradled in the arms of Joseph of Arimithea.

Rembrandt's etching of 1654 takes a different line. The terror and confusion of the crucifixion spills over into this night scene of urgency and fear. A tangle of lines: ladder, cross and torch, makes an edgy contrast to the long linen sling and the struggling bodies. The emphasis is on the dead weight of Christ's body. You can feel that weight in the stance, the braced leg muscles, the strong back, of the man who has taken the body into his arms. Jesus' legs hang loose, one foot is still nailed to the cross awaiting release by the person who seems to gaze thoughtfully at the hammer held in his fingers. Beside him another thrusts forward, dangerously, with a blazing torch. Here again is Rembrandt's signature. The torchlight brings the struggling figures into prominence but leaves the dead Christ's head slipping into shadow. Beyond this, poignantly, the light catches an upraised hand – a man who waits to take the weight of the body or perhaps a woman who had watched Christ die. In the foreground a white shroud is being draped lovingly on a bier. More watchers peer out of the darkness.

Rembrandt is depicting the rituals of death described in the Gospel but he does it at a time and place when death was ever present. He had mourned the deaths of his own wife and two children. He lived in a country where slaughter in civil and religious war was still strong in living memory. As he worked over this etching he could not escape his own experience and it is the same for us. Even if death has not touched us personally, we see and hear it every day, brought into our homes by the same media that allows us to ponder these etchings.

Can I allow myself to enter into the grief of the friends of Jesus at this time? Can I also share the experience of grief in the lives of those around me? In the solidarity of prayer can I open myself to the deaths of the innocent around the world?

Perhaps in the face of this dark mystery all I can do is affirm, in the darkness of faith, the reality of God's love.

THEY CAME BY NIGHT

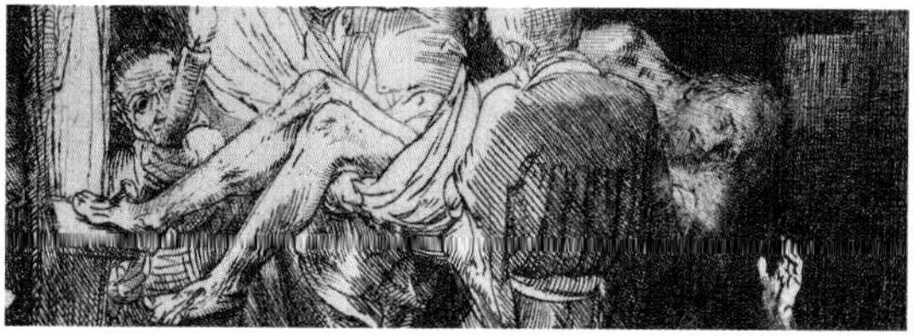

O my chief good,
How shall I measure out thy blood?
How shall I count what thee befell?
And each grief tell?
Then let each hour
Of my whole life one grief devour;
That thy distress through all may run
And be my sun.

FROM *GOOD FRIDAY* BY GEORGE HERBERT
1593-1633

BRINGING MYRRH AND ALOES

THEY REMOVED THE BODY

Rembrandt van RIJN
Dutch 1606-1669
The entombment c.1654
etching, drypoint and burin
21.1 x 15.9 cm
Felton Bequest, 1958

The Entombment

Now there was a garden in the place where Jesus was crucified, and in the garden there was a new tomb in which no one had ever been laid. And so, because it was the Jewish day of Preparation, and the tomb was nearby, they laid Jesus there.

John 19: 41-2

Joseph of Arimathea then rolled a great stone to the door of the tomb and went away. Mary Magdalene and the other Mary were there, sitting opposite the tomb.

Matthew 27: 60-61

They laid Jesus there. In some ways this is the moment of greatest illumination in all Rembrandt's etchings of the life of Christ. And yet it is in almost total darkness. The dark journey of the Flight into Egypt has come home, but to what a home! Yet the friends of Jesus are not in despair. They are calm and expectant.

The composition is harmonious, almost circular, as the eye swings down from the curving arch to the figures on the left, their hands and heads picked out by the light. The light pools over Christ's feet. And rises again through the calm of the sleep of death, and the watching disciples, up to the arch again.

The centre of the picture is a black rectangle, floating and drawing us in ... In so many of these etchings there is a central area of white space – perhaps affirming the Divine Being, who dwells in light. But here the central space is black. This moment between death and resurrection is a dark night in which we let go, of possessions, and of ourselves, so that the mind and the senses reach out to God in the darkness of simple faith.

Matthew's Gospel [27:52] mentions that at this time tombs were opened and the bodies of the saints who had fallen asleep were raised. It is as if time is suspended. Jesus has returned to his father. He has gone to prepare a place, for those who have died, and for us.

Mary Magdalene, or is it Jesus' mother, sits waiting with the others for the tomb to be closed and the stone rolled over. The women will be the first to meet the risen Christ.

THEY LAID JESUS THERE

'O daughters of Jerusalem,
where has your beloved gone?
O fairest among women,
which way has your beloved turned
that we may seek him with you?'
'I come to my garden, my sister, my bride
I gather my myrrh with my spice.'

SONG OF SOLOMON 6:1, 5:1

IN A NEW TOMB

THE WOMEN SAT OPPOSITE

Rembrandt van RIJN

Dutch 1606-1669

Christ at Emmaus: the larger plate 1654

etching, drypoint and burin

20.7 x 16.0 cm

Purchased, 1891

Christ at Emmaus

As the two disciples came near to the village of Emmaus to which they were going, Jesus walked ahead as if he were going on. But they urged him strongly, saying, 'Stay with us, because it is almost evening and the day is now nearly over.' So he went in to stay with them.

When he was at the table with them, he took bread, blessed and broke it, and gave it to them. Then their eyes were opened, and they recognised him; and he vanished from their sight.

They said to each other, 'Were not our hearts burning within us while he was talking to us on the road, while he was opening the scriptures to us?'

That same hour they got up and returned to Jerusalem; and they found the eleven and their companions gathered together. They were saying, 'The Lord has risen indeed and he has appeared to Simon!'

Then they told what had happened on the road, and how he had been made known to them in the breaking of the bread.

Luke 24:28-35

This is one of the most famous images of Christ not only because of Rembrandt's etching but because it recalls the figure of Christ in Leonardo da Vinci's Last Supper which Rembrandt would have known. Although his etchings do not include a Last Supper scene or a Resurrection, this Emmaus picture points us to both.

The central figure of Christ radiates light and calm, even majesty, as he sits facing us under a draped canopy that adds honour – even though the simple furniture and the open arch on the right seem to indicate a humble house. As does the presence of the dog. Is it the house dog looking for scraps of food, or the travellers' dog grateful for shelter? Or perhaps a reference to the dogs that eat the crumbs that fall from the master's table? [Matthew 15: 27]

The two disciples and the inn-keeper are caught in the moment of recognition as Jesus breaks the bread and opens out his arms to them and to us.

By the time this story was recorded in Luke's Gospel the followers of Jesus would have been celebrating his memory in a thanksgiving meal, sharing bread and wine as a sign of his presence among them. The Emmaus story thus reminds us of Christ's death and of his Resurrection. It shows the triumph of love that overcame the grim scenes of the passion of Christ. This meal is a sign of unity and love.

As I read the story and look at the picture I join with all who celebrate Christ's memory. I seat myself at the table – and I watch the hands that break the bread. I share the wonder, the faith, the hope and joy of the disciples at Emmaus. From now on I recognise every shared meal as an Emmaus encounter. Every chance meeting along the way is a meeting with Jesus, a pathway to prayer, an opportunity for love.

STAY WITH US LORD

Generous God of all goodness,
nourish us along the way of our exile,
until we come to contemplate
the face of Christ our Lord,
no longer veiled, but moving
from glory to glory,
transformed by the breath
of your sweet Spirit.

GERTRUDE OF HELFTA, 1289

OUR HEARTS WERE BURNING WITHIN US

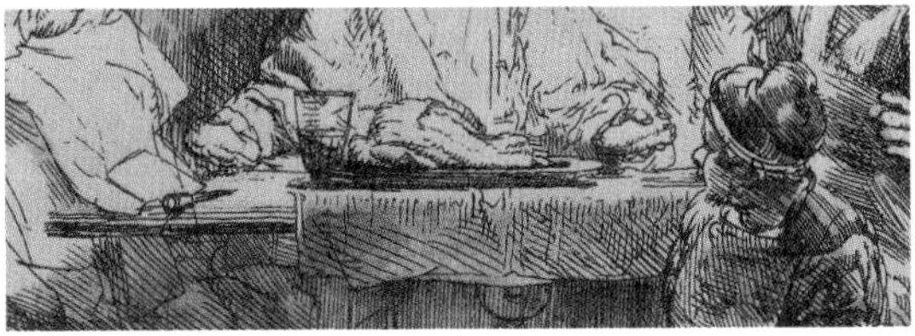

WE KNEW HIM IN THE BREAKING OF THE BREAD

Chronology of the Life of Rembrandt

1606 Rembrandt born at Leiden in Holland, 15 July, the son of a miller.

1621 After attending the Latin school and briefly, Leiden University, Rembrandt became an apprentice painter.

1624 Spent six months in Amsterdam and returned to Leiden.

1626 Began sharing a studio with painter, Jan Lievens. First etchings begun around this time.

1630 Rembrandt's father died.

1631 Moved to Amsterdam and quickly became the city's most famous portrait painter.

1632 Etched *The Raising of Lazarus: The Larger Plate* .

1634 Married Saskia van Uylenburgh (b.1612). Early paintings of the life of Christ.

1635–36 Birth and death of first son, Rombertus.

1637 Acquired many works of art.

1638 Birth and death of daughter, Cornelia. Accused by his wife's relatives of squandering her inheritance.

1639 Bought a large house on the Breestraat for which he went into debt.

1640 Birth and death of his second daughter, also Cornelia. Rembrandt's mother died 14 September.

1641–42 Birth of son Titus, the only child to reach adulthood. Saskia died 14 June, 1642, leaving her inheritance to Titus, to be managed by Rembrandt except in the case that he remarried. Geertge Dircx entered the house as Titus's nurse. Rembrandt commissioned to paint his most famous group portrait, *The Nightwatch*.

1648 Geertge Dircx willed her property to Titus and sued Rembrandt for breach of promise of marriage. She was put in a reformatory and her place taken by Hendrickje Stoffels.

1654 Hendrickje was brought before an ecclesiastical court and accused of concubinage. A daughter, Cornelia, born some months later.

1655 Geertge Dircx released after litigations against Rembrandt.

1656 Rembrandt applies for voluntary bankruptcy.

1657–58 House and possessions auctioned to pay creditors. He remains on premises two more years.

1660–61 Rembrandt, Hendrickje and children move to a smaller house.

1663 Hendrickje died.

1665 Titus came of age and claimed his share of proceeds of bankruptcy sales.

1668–69 Titus married Magdalena van Loo, 10 February. He died 4 September. Rembrandt painted *The Jewish Bride, The Return of the Prodigal Son,* and *Simeon Holding the Infant Christ*.

1669 Baptism of Titia, Titus's posthumously born daughter, 22 March. Rembrandt died, 4 October 1669.

Acknowledgements

My thanks to Dr Claire Renkin whose lectures in Art and Spirituality at the Yarra Theological Union campus of the Melbourne College of Divinity have been the inspiration for this book. Also to friends among Dominican Associates and in the parishes of Ferntree Gully and Boronia who have shared with me their lives and prayer. I am especially grateful to John Petrulis PP, Frank Gerry SVD and to Barbara Kenny for their comments and suggestions.

The author and the publisher also wish to thank the following for permission to reproduce material in this book. The Trustees of the National Gallery of Victoria for permission to reproduce the Rembrandt etchings. Michael Leunig for the prayer on page 105

The prayer on page 45 is from the hymn, *Lieber Jesu, Wir Sind Hier* by Tobias Clausnitzner, 1619-84, translated by Catherine Winkworth, 1827-78. There is a setting of the hymn in *The Australian Hymn Book*, Collins, Sydney 2001, no.352.

The prayer on page 77 is from the hymn, *Jesu Rex Admirabilis* attributed to St Bernard of Clairvaux, 1091-1153, translated by Edward Caswall 1814-78. Musical setting in *The Australian Hymn Book* no.1125.

The following publications provided background and information about Rembrandt:

Carroll, M. Deutsch. *'Rembrandt as Meditational Printmaker'*. *Art Bulletin,* LXIII(4), December 1981, 585-610

Gregory, John and Zdanowicz, Irena. *Rembrandt in the Collections of the National Gallery of Victoria*. Published by the National Gallery of Victoria, Melbourne, 1988

Schama, Simon, *Rembrandt's Eyes*, Penguin, 1999.

THE AUTHOR

ANNE MARGOT BOYD is an Australian who, in 1955, joined the Dominican contemplative community at Carisbrooke on the Isle of Wight, England. She was one of the founders of Carisbrooke Priory Press which flourished in the 1960s. In 1968 she moved to Cambridge where she worked for thirteen years in the publishing division of Cambridge University Press. In the 1980s she edited the Geoffrey Chapman list of Catholic theology, liturgy and catechetics for Cassell Publishers in London. In 1989 she returned to Australia where she now lives, combining freelance editing and writing with MA research on paintings of Catherine of Siena.